BRAIN
SURGERY
THE BOOK

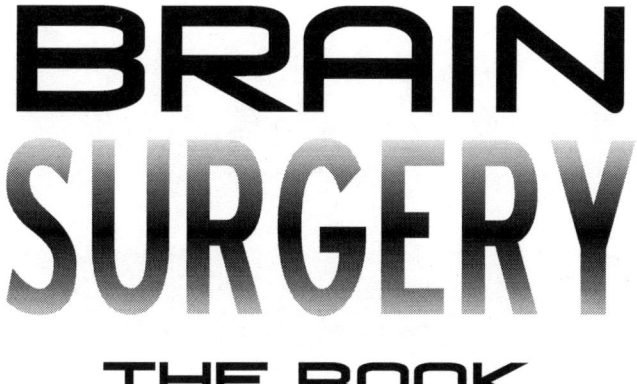

King D Son

Copyright © 2015 by King D Son.

Library of Congress Control Number: 2015908793
ISBN: Hardcover   978-1-5035-7525-7
         Softcover   978-1-5035-7524-0
         eBook   978-1-5035-7523-3

All rights reserved. No part of this book may be reproduced or transmitted in any form or by any means, electronic or mechanical, including photocopying, recording, or by any information storage and retrieval system, without permission in writing from the copyright owner.

Any people depicted in stock imagery provided by Thinkstock are models, and such images are being used for illustrative purposes only.
Certain stock imagery © Thinkstock.

Print information available on the last page.

Rev. date: 06/02/2015

To order additional copies of this book, contact:
Xlibris
1-888-795-4274
www.Xlibris.com
Orders@Xlibris.com
715035

INTRODUCTION

My name is Darius Southerland. I also go by the name King D Son, though only when entertainment is involved. I write movie scripts as well. I've made a short film called *We All We Got*. I was born and raised in Nashville, Tennessee. My mother has six kids: four boys and two girls. I lived in the ghetto all my life. "I learned that keeping the faith always overpower the dark nights filled with pain."

Chapter One

THE HELPING HAND

Never overdose on trying to be a good person. You're only setting yourself up for failure. Most people are needy, and they will be around you until your last penny is gone. The only reward you will get for being the helping hand is people turning their backs when you need them the most. Look at the world for what it is and not for what you would want it to be. It is better that you be hated for the person you are than to be loved for the person you're not.

Do not give people the key to your mind because they will change the lock on you and control it. Never say things you don't mean; it's only going to hurt you in the end. The people who only say things because the moment is right will never have respect because it only looks like you don't believe in yourself and people will find it harder to trust you.

Making mistakes is human nature, but not learning from them can set up rocky roads ahead. So find your purpose and rebuild your life or you can blame no one for your actions but yourself.

I'm not saying helping people is a bad thing. I've helped out a lot of people. All I'm saying is "don't change who you are just because you want people to like you, and if you are afraid to use the word *no,* your career will go nowhere." You can't be afraid to tell people you can't do something. Saying yes all the time will make you seem like a pushover, and you will not get respect this way.

I understand nobody wants to look mean or to be mistaken as a bad person, and I honestly feel like you should want people to talk behind your back. That means they respect you enough to not say it in your face. Nobody controls your life but you. So if you're feeling sad or hurt, either it's time to cut people off or change your life without letting the fear hold you back.

Chapter Two
LIVING WITH DEPRESSION

Depression starts from the way you think. If you dwell on anything for too long in a negative way, it causes depression. If a person doesn't like you just because they hate themselves, you'll be confused. You may begin to put pieces together yourself to have a better understanding, but all you're doing is trying to figure something out that's not fixable. You're not going to always have an answer to your problem.

Some people will never say they're sorry for hurting you. This is something you'll have to live with. I'm not saying don't try to fix it. If you think you can be a big help to why things is the way they are, go for, it but do not dwell on something that's not approachable.

Nobody wants to be disliked, but some people will have issues with you without a reason. Just move forward because sometimes problems fix themselves. People say bad things about me everywhere

I go. It hurts because I'm human, but I will not dwell on it at all. I take it for what it is and move on because I know if I worry, that will only lead to stress, and stress leads to depression.

I prefer that people stay active as much as possible. When things are going wrong, it may not fix the problem, but you're molding your thoughts to think differently. Basically, all you need to do is take out your pain on something that you love to do. If you are a singer, go into the studio and record a song about the things you don't understand, and then sell the project. This is called selling your past to better your future, and you'll see how all your problems turned into success. So thank the ones who put you through different struggles because without rain, there's no growth.

Chapter Three

THE PRESSURE OF BEING JUDGED

Normally, when people are judgmental, they often feel bad about themselves. Think of them as bank robbers; normally, things start to go wrong in their lives, and then stress starts developing around their minds, and that leads to frustration. This is when the hunt is on, and they start making other people feel the pain that they're feeling.

But judgmental people are not robbing you of money. They're robbing you of your self-respect. You see, what they're doing is looking for people they admire the most or the ones they feel can actually make it far in life. Then they try to destroy everything that they believe in.

Think about it, why kill someone's spirit who doesn't believe in himself or herself. That's like robbing somebody who you know doesn't have money; that'll be a waste of time. So what they do is they will seek the ones who have major faith in God just so they can strip them down to zero. And the moment they notice that you're off balance, now it's their time to tell the world it's you who have the problem, not them.

There've been times I couldn't sleep at night because I was so stressed out. I was paying too much attention on how people felt about me. I never knew how to use my strength until I was put in a situation, and I had no choice. You can be a sweet person with a heart made of gold, and people will still judge you. Don't let the thoughts of others control your actions. If you're afraid to grow in life just because of the fear of what someone else may think, then you are moments from failure.

Think about it for a second; let's say you get a traffic ticket, and then you'll be judged by a person who wasn't even there when the situation took place. This world has at least 80 percent of people who are judgmental. If there's no way around them, you'll have to deal with the pressure of being judged. But it doesn't define who you are as a person. Just move forward no matter what, and eventually, you'll learn how to live with it.

Chapter Four

KNOWING YOUR SELF-WORTH

When young kids reach the age of thirteen or fourteen, making choices can become very difficult. Around that age, it's more about image because at that age, they basically have nothing to live for at the moment. Cleaning up their room and taking out the trash is most likely the biggest job they have. Even if the child is being raised by both parents, they will still follow the world because 70 percent of the world cherishes the things kids glorify.

On one end, mom and dad are saying go to school, but on the other end, the young child is no longer paying attention to what the parents are saying because they feel the world teaches them things they can relate to. If the world makes it seem like going to school is for dummies, then most kids will not be happy with going. Just because children don't know their self-worth does not mean your child is a bad kid. Maybe they're afraid of being themselves—the fear of not fitting in—and that allows them to make the same mistakes repeatedly.

But adults have the same issues; just think about it. There are a lot of street guys who are very smart, but if judgmental people see them carrying books in their hands, they will make them feel like they're trying to be better than them. So the smart guys put their wisdom to the side to hang out with people with no future, all because they're not fitting in. Some people will go broke just to look rich; never change who you are just to make someone look at you in a good way.

Chapter Five
ONE-SIDED MIND

If you are the type of person who only thinks one-sided, life can be very difficult. If you only like to hang out with people who look, talk, and dress like you, the length of your future goals will be limited to the way you think. Even if the one-sided person is wrong, they will fight to be right. Explaining the way you feel to these types of people will never work; you are clearly wasting your time.

You have to understand that those people are not very strong-minded. They see wrong in anything, and whatever it takes to get their point across, they will do it, even if it makes them look immature. The one-sided persons talk very loud and act very bold, but deep in their soul, there's only unhappiness that their pride will never show.

If you think they're ever going to be the bigger person in the situation, stop thinking about it because it's not going to happen. And it's very sad if you have to live this way because every day you'll have to pretend to be something that you're not, and that can be a hard job.

Have you ever seen people who need help but they're always thinking someone else needs help because they don't want to admit the truth about themselves? The one thing they don't realize is that they're only hurting themselves. Think about it, do you know how long you'll have to be angry or selfish every day? Look at the amount of energy that you're wasting just to prove something.

If these people think more positive, they will understand how many friends they've lost due to their lack of knowledge. Train your mind to become the bigger adult about life issues; learn talking instead of yelling. The only result that comes with wanting to be noticed is failure.

Chapter Six

MISUNDERSTOOD

People who think they're misunderstood most likely feel they weren't given a fair chance. If you apply pressure to a good person, their attitude will change. For example, people with a good heart normally do not like confrontation. So they have no problem being the bigger person in any situation.

Good-hearted people are often taken for granted. Most people think they are weak-minded human beings. Most of the time, the people who are misunderstood like to smile and brush things off or simply just ignore them. They also can appear shy, but if they are comfortable around you, they'll be very open. But in the meantime, they just observe and listen. And they think before speaking; that's why they can point out things that will hurt you directly because the whole time they've been watching.

But you cannot confuse a good-hearted person then expect them to think clearly. That's like not hiring me for a job when you have ten positions open and get upset because I choose to make money elsewhere. To me, that's having control on both sides.

So if good-hearted people decided to leave you alone completely, it's only because they didn't want to feel controlled. But could you really be mad at them for protecting themselves? And if you are mad, then it clearly shows you're more in love with feeling the power of being selfish than loving the person you actually said you cared for.

Take a look in the mirror and ask yourself: Do I love myself? Am I really happy with who I am as a person? And if the answer is *no*, then maybe someone is being the victim of your failure. Does this sound like you? Do the people around you really deserve to be misunderstood? Have you taken the time out to listen to the way they feel, or do you listen with the intention of not paying attention? Do you have the mind that thinks like regardless if they right their wrong?

Always go through the different steps with yourself before giving someone the feeling of being misunderstood. The world does not work from your point of view. Think about it, would you be upset if people never gave you a chance to be heard? Learn more about respect because you're taking personal feelings out on the people who will give you their last dollar. But if you can't see that, then maybe it's only because you're too busy thinking about yourself.

Chapter Seven

THE KEY TO FAILURE

Taking the blame for other people's mistakes is one of the fastest ways to failure. Also being too nice sometimes may cause mental damage; never allow the way you feel about someone lead you to self-destruct.

But God somehow always gives us signs, and we all have been at fault by ignoring them. And later in life, we all say the same thing: I should have listened, or why did I do that when I knew better?

Let your past be your past; but it's OK to look at where you went wrong. Just focus more on your new plans and realize that every smiling face isn't happy. Sometimes we look at people and don't want to believe the truth because of the love we have for them. But I've been in situations like this, and they never end well.

We get upset at the people we feel should appreciate us more, but then we ignore the people who does. Everyone is not for you; some people will forget everything you've ever done for them. I'm not saying care less; just learn how to love from afar, and don't be afraid to let go of people. Stop watering things that wasn't meant to grow in your life; take all the energy that you put in others and put it back in yourself. Rebuild your self-esteem; you are in control of your own life and responsible for your own actions. Eventually, you'll have to stop pointing your finger and realize every choice you make is yours.

Chapter Eight

POSITIVE VERSUS NEGATIVE

Sometimes being positive can feel almost impossible to do at times because the world is so negative. There are some people in life who are doing good, meaning they have a job, a nice car, and their own house. It's amazing how they can still be jealous-hearted toward a person that's not doing so good. But if you're honest with your struggle and realize things do change as long as you keep the faith, you'll find more people being attached to you because it's not the struggle that they see, it's something on the inside of you that could only be created by God himself.

But negative people with small minds could never understand why people are so attached to a person without money. The reason is because everything is not looked at from a cynical point of view. Understand that negative people hate themselves. That's why they try to bring others down to their level. Some people get a kick out of watching other people suffer.

And then there are people who like to show off even if they cannot afford the things they have. About 90 percent of their focus is image, so when they talk reality with you, it's only coming from a 10 percent point of view. They're not sensible at all. That's why they get so aggressive and easily quit anything that requires patience. So when they see other people doing the things they don't have the time for, the situation can become very critical.

Negative people hate to lose, and a person who's afraid to lose will do anything to win. The best way to beat them at their own game is to ignore everything they throw at you. They do not know how to react with something that's not fighting back. It confuses them because they feed off battles, and they will starve if there are no battles to fight. And anything starved for too long will die. So your job is to kill them with success and bury them with a smile.

Chapter Nine

THE FEAR OF CHANGE

The fear of change comes from being afraid of acceptance. Your thoughts are one of the most, if not the most important, attachments that come with human nature. Life is bigger than just reality and the way things look. If you can set your mind to see the invisible, then you can do the impossible.

There are seven days in one week; let's say today is Monday, and you slept all day, and then Tuesday comes. There's no way you can ask God if he can rewind back to yesterday because you forgot to do something. Basically, what I'm saying is no matter what you didn't get to do today, you'll just have to make up for it the next day because God is not going backward for no one.

All I'm saying is continue to move forward; it's the only way to better yourself. And stop living in the past. There's nothing there, though there have been times we all lost a loved one and wish we can go back to that day. I understand that it hurts. But how would you know the strength you had if you don't move forward? If things never move forward in life, our kids will be children forever. What would be the point of teaching them right from wrong if they're never going to use it? But your kids will find a way to move forward even if you, as parents, are at a standstill because the world doesn't work off fear; it works off movement.

Chapter Ten

LIVING ON SOMEONE ELSE'S THOUGHTS

If someone can change your mind on how you should feel about others, they also have the ability to make you turn against yourself. For example, if I pay you to fight someone that I don't like, it's either because I don't know how to stop that person myself or I'm too afraid to get my own hands dirty.

If you love the person they're sending you out to attack, your approach is going to be with caution because you know how good they've been to you. So as you begin the attack, your heart is hurting because you know deep down they don't deserve it. And your body will start feeling dysfunctional. Why? It's because you're targeting someone who treated you with love.

But all this means you are living someone else's thoughts. People who think evil against other people always find others to manipulate because they cannot fight their battles alone. Remember, it's all a trick just to get you to hate the people they dislike, and sometimes they have no true purpose for not liking others. It can all be because they hate how their own life is going. And they also create pressure for themselves and realize the pain is too much, so they find other people to send out to fight their battles. Not only will they have you attack the ones you love, but they will also have you fight without a good reason. At the end, you'll see how much failure this game can actually bring you.

Remember, people with negative minds only adapt to things they can see; they could never understand the invisible love of having a dream or to be patient with future hopes. They don't think before they speak, but they do show actions before they think. These people will treat you bad today and smile in your face tomorrow. You cannot trust them, and never believe anything they say even if it sounds good because everything they do comes with a trick.

Chapter Eleven

BE HONEST IN YOUR MUSIC

Artists who tell lies in their music are basically stealing respect. For example, if you are an artist who releases songs about things you've done but they're all lies, you are putting your fans at risk. This is because people who don't know you personally can only respect you from what they hear in your music.

I'm not saying you're responsible for everybody's actions, but it doesn't help by you lying in your music. Because fans take what you say to heart, and if you're speaking in your music like you're violent, then your fans will expect to see you act that way in person.

So it's very important for you to watch what you say. If you are not the person you are in the studio, I really think you need to change careers fast. Basically, all that I'm saying is to be honest with yourself so you can receive the respect you deserve. It is not OK for artists to lie to the fans.

Think about this: If your fans do react off what you are speaking about, it's because you're making them feel it's cool to be violent. The music business is all about money, and some of these big-time executives put you out as an artist who looks like having a lot of money. Never allow a record label to have you in a situation where you can end up being hurt or losing your career due to lying. Always tell the truth no matter how large the amount of money being offered.

Chapter Twelve
THE RACE TO FAME

We're living in a world that's 60 percent brainwashed. Most people think that when you become famous, all your problems go away. I hear people talk all the time about being successful because most of their ideas of having fame is being on top of the world.

But in a sense, you're right. You should want it all; that's called ambition. But not knowing how to keep what you've earned is called lack of knowledge. Even if you are a strong-minded person, make sure all your steps are calculated. Never allow your mind to think it's a competition against others because if you do, then everything you've created is seconds from failure.

Let the others race to the top. It's always best to make plans and then move at the right time because it eliminates many mistakes you would've made if you rushed. Never be afraid to learn new things; keeping your mind open helps you to figure out obstacles when they're in the way.

Some people might think evil things toward you just to keep you off balance, and they also want you to see things the way they want you to see it. The longer you learn how to stay in your lane, the better off you'll be. Never follow trends; always create your own. Be willing to walk with patience because having an understanding about the business that you're in is way better than just being a part of it.

If you have a vision, always keep that vision; don't settle for something less than what you're worth. The fame is going to come, but some people are so much in a rush that they're willing to sell their soul just to have the feeling of everybody loving them. But if you're weak in that way, then guess what. Your fifteen minutes of fame will only last for five. So believe in yourself, rich or broke. Just know that your worth is more than just a race to fame.

Chapter Thirteen
MIND POWER

Having mind control is very important; your brain is like the motor to your car. And without the proper thinking, the body is dead. Think about it. If you wash your car and put brand new tires on it but the engine is bad, the most you can do is tell yourself what you could've done today was just take pictures of the car because you like the way it looks.

All that I'm saying is don't worry so much about the image. Most people think wearing the best clothes will make people trust them more. All it does is bring attention to persons that's going to embarrass themselves if they don't have the knowledge to go with their look.

For example, if I committed a crime and I preferred to wear a suit to court and if I'm found guilty, will the judge say, "I'm going to let you go because I like your suit." *No*, I'll have a better chance of getting a not guilty plea if myself or my lawyer have the knowledge to argue my case about citizens' rights. You know why? This is so because it's 10 percent image and 90 percent knowledge.

That brings me to my second point: Learn how to mold your thinking, and what I mean is take your anger out on positive things. Because it's so easy to get upset and do things you'll later regret, molding your mind is doing things in an opposite way. If you get upset at someone, instead of fighting, just walk off. I'm not saying be a pussy and don't defend yourself. But doing things in opposite ways will keep people off balance. They wouldn't know what you're thinking.

If you know someone doesn't like you, play stupid and smile at them and joke with them. Thinking like this will not only make people feel bad about themselves. It will also keep you from being stressed as well.

But this whole world is controlled by the way people think. Listen to me. Everything in your house came from a thought that someone had. Somebody was thinking, *Man, how can I make a heater when it's cold outside? Or if I wanted to wire money to my daughter, how could I come up with a plan to create such things?*

Every single thing built on this earth comes from a thought, so if your mind is not creating something as we speak, then there's someone thinking how they can use you to work for them since you don't have a mind of your own. I'm not saying working for somebody is a bad thing. I'm just saying figure out a way to get them to work for you.

Chapter Fourteen

GOOD HEART, NO MONEY

I come from a place where loyalty runs thin, and what I mean is some people have their own way of looking at life. They might feel like it doesn't matter how real you are. If you don't have money, you're nobody. With this type of pressure on, you will only be left with two choices, either you keep it real no matter what people think or you try to fit in even if it means selling your soul.

I chose to be real, so with that been said, I received a lot of hate. Some people say negative things, hoping it will allow my mind to agree with what they feel. And yes, words do hurt especially when they're coming from people to whom you gave all.

And some people look at failure in a bad way; it depends on how you read the situation. I think failure is not good, but it does have great things that comes along with it, like knowing who your real friends are and seeing how people treat you once you've taken a loss.

You would never see this if you were always doing good because everybody would be around you showing love. I thank God for my struggles because when I do get rich, it will be easy to separate the people who care and who don't. Of course, it's going to hurt you when you realize all the love you thought you had you really don't, and yes, you're going to cry, and you also might feel like you can't make it on your own. But all these things come with struggling. But if you can survive the pain, then God is going to do some wonderful things in your life.

You might hear people say you can't or you're never going to prosper. Just teach yourself to ignore the hate and focus on your main goals. Remember, everybody is not going to like you; don't think you're going to be loved everywhere you go. Fifty percent of the time, they are going to hate you because you're great at what you do and you have dreams.

Most of the people who dislike you do not have dreams. They cannot see what you see and feel you're chasing something that's never going to happen, but keep chasing your dreams anyway. They want you to give up so they can feel everything they said about you was true. But don't argue with those types of people; it's a waste of time. Just let your career do the talking, and if you're winning, they will have no choice but to respect your accomplishments.

Chapter Fifteen
BRAIN DEAD

Brain dead is my definition of saying your mind is not controlled by you. If someone has the ability to control your mind, it doesn't matter how much money you have, because it will always be that one person who can take you back to square one, all because you are not in control of your own mind.

How can you better yourself if your legs are moving but your mind is still stuck in the same place? You cannot be here and trying to go there at the same time. People will control your thoughts longer if you allow them to; it's up to you to make that change. If you're afraid to prosper, you will lose so much in the process.

Sometimes life doesn't give you a time to change. Sometimes you'll have to just go where your heart tell you to. I've been at points in my life when I didn't have time to get it right; I just had to change. I didn't know what I'll get out of changing. I didn't have a plan. I didn't know if I was going to fail; all I knew was it was time to change.

You cannot let people scare you so much that you refuse to grow. If you're the type of person who just likes to talk about how you want things to be but you're not doing anything to make it happen, you're clearly wasting your time. Because you cannot cheat life; you can lie to me, but you cannot cheat life because life has no feelings, and it will give you what you paid for.

Life will put you around people with *no* goals if you're the type who just talk about how things should be. Why would you complain about who are around you? It's all about what you want out of life. But one thing for sure, if you keep allowing people to have control over your mind, then you might as well be brain dead.

Chapter Sixteen

DIRTY DIAMOND

I'm from the ghetto. I grew up broke. My father left me when I was three years old. I sold drugs, and I dropped out of school. As you can tell from the things I've mentioned, my life was far from perfect. But some people will look at your struggles and lose hope on you; they feel you don't deserve a second chance with anything. When they all turned their backs on me, it made me feel like I was to blame, and it almost made me feel like it was a bad thing to struggle.

But as I think about it, I realized, no matter how hard you worked or how far you go in life, there will always be struggle. Some people are broke at this moment, but they will not say they're broke. You see, to me, that's like being embarrassed of something that was here before we were born. Life made me accept my situation, and what I mean is you'll have to adapt to your struggle to make it.

Certain answers that you need in order to survive are only found deep inside the struggle, but you will never understand if you're the type who always pretend. I think people misunderstood me when I said I had to accept my struggle; I guess it made them feel like I was saying I'm OK with being broke. But that's not what I was saying; I just found a way that I can struggle without thinking I'm cursed for being in the hood.

I still feel God has more for me to do. I know deep down I'm still a diamond I just have a little dirt on me, so at times it's hard to see it shine. If the sun had a dark cloud around it, it doesn't mean it's not going to shine again. It just has to finish the stormy situation first. If you like to judge people who're going through a storm, I feel sorry for you because your struggle is going to be harder than the person you pointed your finger at.

Chapter Seventeen

SHE'S DOING THE BEST SHE CAN

I've watched my mother survive alone with six kids. Some nights, she didn't eat. We were poor, so at times we went without water and food. With the amount of stress that she was bearing, I couldn't do it. So with that being said, I'll always support her. But the struggle doesn't stop with my mother; this is going on around the world. I have a major respect for women. Neither I nor any man on earth could imagine the pain women have to deal with.

Think about it this way, that close brother you love so much came from a woman's womb. Or look at it in a deeper way; every person on earth that you see came from a woman's womb. If it weren't for women, this world would be lost. Don't get me wrong; a man can take care of himself, but a woman can make you feel a different kind of special.

It's only 40 percent of what men can do that women can't, but it's 60 percent of what women can do that men can't. I'm not saying they're better human beings, but I am saying they're great. Because a woman can take care of her kids with no job and no car, but one thing is for sure, the job is going to get done.

I just want the world to know how beautiful women are on the inside and out. I learn from them a lot. Just try talking to your wife or girlfriend about some of the things they deal with, I guarantee you'll be shocked.

Could you imagine giving birth to another human being and carrying them around for nine months? That's a hard thing to do; extra weight on them. Their backs are hurting all the time, but us men become upset only because we can't watch the game. Just listen to her side of the story. I know at times it can get hard because women are emotional, and they can be a ticking time bomb. But just try if you can, because she's doing the best she can do.

Chapter Eighteen

THE THREE STEPS OF LIFE

There are three crucial steps in life that you'll have to survive. It doesn't matter if you're good or bad. These steps will leave you stressed and confused, but if you're willing to accept the challenge, then understand that it will also mold you to become a better and stronger person that's filled with knowledge and wisdom.

STEP 1: It's called verbal abuse. There will be people who'd say negative things that will hurt your feelings. For example, you can't make it on your own or you're better off dead. Some of those words will come from people you care about the most, but this step you're taking will make you feel like people hate you and that they lost faith in you, and at times, it will be so stressful that you'll want to give up. But this is helping to gain strength in places you never had before. If you're still willing to fight and not give up, then this brings me to my next point.

STEP 2: This is called physical abuse. Now this is where it gets a little more difficult. Verbal abuse is still going on as you deal with physical abuse. This step is when people set traps for you to fall and lose everything you've created. This is when jealousy comes and people not only say things like they want you dead, but they actually try to kill you themselves. They might see that you are doing good in life, so now they want to rob you or start trouble with you so you can react in a violent way. They also will apply so much pressure on you to the point that you'll have to buy guns just to survive. They will do anything to keep you off balance, because they know words cannot stop you. But just know through the process of physical abuse that you should not lose your cool. There might be times when you'll have to protect yourself, but keep your mind focused on the bigger picture. But this is only a test, and if you're still willing to fight, then this brings me to my next point.

STEP 3: This is called mental abuse, one of the hardest steps of them all. Don't think that because you've overcome verbal and physical abuse, it's over. You will feel the physical abuse, and you will also feel the verbal abuse. As you enter this new step, you will have to understand that dealing with mental abuse is all about a mind game. For example, picture someone or you being brain dead. Even if you're able to move your legs and feet, your body will still not move. And mental abuse is almost the same as being brain dead. This is because people will play mind games with you to the point you know longer know yourself. Everything you hate about yourself comes from the person who's been brainwashing you. They're teaching you that you cannot make it in life without them, and if they get you to a stage in your life where you're afraid of falling, then they got you. But it doesn't mean it's over for you. At least you'll be able to move your legs, but are you able to control you own thoughts? This step is called mental abuse, and it's so serious that if you lose your way, it's very easy to become a victim of someone else's failure. Because some people are so weak, they have to blame others for their mistakes. If they see a person who's lost, they'll be more than happy to find you a home. Yes, you'll eat, but you can't control your mind. And yes, you'll be comfortable, but you can't control your mind. It's almost like being homeless with a place to stay. So please control your own mind because the struggle involved in these steps will pay off.

Chapter Nineteen

THE DIFFERENT THINKER

Thinking different is not always a bad thing. Look at it in a way that God has chosen you to make an impact on the world that only you can do. But sometimes the chosen persons are afraid to be different, so they include themselves with people who are not chosen. But it's much easier to be yourself than to pretend.

Think about this: If you're the type to pretend, and people adapt to you, could you honestly say you've earned the love you got? In the way that the world is in today, you should want to think differently. Let's look at it like this: Say if people go left, then you should go right.

If people are making too much music about violence, then you make music about something a little softer. If you follow what I've shown you, I promise people are going to come and tell you how you inspired them, all because you're different.

I look at it like this: People can't get tired of something they're not used to having. Find out what everybody is doing, and then do the opposite, especially if you're into creating a business. For the most part, just never be afraid to believe in yourself.

I'm not telling you to be a sellout for the fame or selling your soul just to be different. All that I'm saying is sometimes you will have to use common sense because this whole world is programmed.

The government manipulates the lower class by convincing them that Section 8 is the best way to go. Basically, what I'm saying is the government gives away free rent or low-income housing to keep us thinking this is all we're worth. This is because they know that the longer they keep the rent at $50 a month, you're not going to be comfortable anywhere else, and in your mind you're probably thinking, "Why would I move?" I understand if you're in this situation, and you have no choice but to get government help. But all I'm saying is just know that everything is a business, and you wouldn't understand if you choose to think like everyone else.

THE END

THANKS FOR GIVING ME THE CHANCE TO SHOW YOU ANOTHER WAY.

LOVE YOU ALL

Rosegal.com

Edwards Brothers Malloy
Oxnard, CA USA
July 24, 2015